Do Not Forsake Me

poems by

Alec Solomita

Finishing Line Press
Georgetown, Kentucky

Do Not Forsake Me

Copyright © 2017 by Alec Solomita
ISBN 978-1-63534-312-0 First Edition
All rights reserved under International and Pan-American Copyright Conventions.
No part of this book may be reproduced in any manner whatsoever without written
permission from the publisher, except in the case of brief quotations embodied in critical
articles and reviews.

ACKNOWLEDGMENTS

Thank you to the editors of the publications in which the following poems first appeared, sometimes in slightly different forms and sometimes differently titled.

"Walking Home" originally published in *Algebra of Owls*
"In the Penal Colony" originally published in *Driftwood Press*
"Raptor" originally published in *Far Off Places*
"Rattus Rattus" originally published in *MockingHeart Review*
"Dog Day Cigarette" originally published in *Panoplyzine*
"Blight" originally published in *The Poeming Pigeon: The Poetry Box*
"Barbecue" originally published in *The Sourland Mountain Review*
"Bertha You Are Not" originally published in the *South Florida Poetry Journal*
"Your Hair's Sour Scent" originally published in *Turk's Head Review*

For their sage, sensitive, and lively advice as I struggled with this book, I'd like to thank Emily Axelrod, Georgia Bellas, Frannie Lindsay, Elliot Scott Slater, Leah Xue, and, especially, Katia Kapovich.

Publisher: Leah Maines

Editor: Christen Kincaid

Cover Art and Design: Alec Solomita

Author Photo: Alec Solomita

Printed in the USA on acid-free paper.
Order online: www.finishinglinepress.com
also available on amazon.com

Author inquiries and mail orders:
Finishing Line Press
P. O. Box 1626
Georgetown, Kentucky 40324
U. S. A.

Table of Contents

Dog Day Cigarette 1
'Grief Hangs Heavy Over Danvers High' 2
Brunch 3
Autumn Fruit 4
The Click of the Door 5
Missing 6
All This Time 7
Raptor 8
The Evening Wolves 9
Bertha You Are Not 10
Walking Home 11
Your Hair's Sour Scent 12
Agador 13
Rattus Rattus 14
Your Words 15
Dancer 16
'Sunshine' 17
It's a Strange Thing 18
Do Not Forsake Me 19
Blight 21
In the Penal Colony 22
Parting 23
Pollyanna 24
Friends like You 25
Barbecue 26

For Joan

Dog Day Cigarette

On the back step
in the green pulse of crickets
by the rusting Weber

while the neighbors
play catch among
the statuary

and ailing wives
are quiet for a spell
and even talk radio

on the other side
goes silent,

I smoke,
the blue evening relaxes,
and a slight shift

in the breeze
sifts out a fine fragment
of unappeasable winter.

'Grief Hangs Heavy Over Danvers High'

The condo glows like a realtor's brochure.
Late October light is clean and brisk like
the Spanish across the street where the builders
climb up ladders leaning against unborn condos,
priming, painting, tacking tiles.

"Grief hangs heavy over Danvers High"
alliterates the Herald, and so it does
and always will, over somewhere.
The headline, the grief, are congenial
to our glowing home. Except for the
hammering—hollow, then high-pitched—
and the Latino staccato at the nascent condos,

all is silence. Silent shifting on the sofa we
shopped for so carefully before we knew
you were ill. Silent rustling of paper as
I read an interview with John Hollander
I barely attend. Attention must be paid

and I'm out of liquid assets except the
lachrymose, as Hollander would surely
never write. Realtors talk about a starter
home and I joked from the start about our
ender home. And nothing's funny any more.
And grief hangs heavy over Danvers High.

Brunch

By the time I noticed the couple of smirky lean
college boys watching you claw your Reuben,
I was too tired to want to kill them. Normally
I'd want to kill them just for being young and tall and rich.
But now, despite their disdain, their careless amusement
at you in this slightly fancy café eating with your fingers,
open mouthed, pulling at corned beef and rye like
a rustic boor, I don't have the energy to kill.

I don't have the energy to be ashamed
any more. I'm just grateful if you
don't stain your blouse again, with mustard
this time, you poor old darling you, who pauses between
chews to ask what we're having for dinner.

Autumn Fruit

Time passes like a slow cloud in August
this November afternoon. It's Sunday
and today's treat for the great disappearing
wife is roasted pumpkin seeds (*graines brûlée!*).

My mom used to make these babies for us
and I've brought her back via pumpkin,
lodging the point of the blade with care so it
won't slip with the hard push through the skin.

Sugar pumpkin the kid said is best for seeds
and my old sweetheart watches like a kid
as I pick through the pumpkin brains, the wet
fibrous strands, the pulp under the orange lid

of the fruit. A half-century blows by
like breeze-torn clouds in winter,
the ancient aroma rising like
blackbirds from the oiled pan, a dish dainty

enough to set before a queen,
one-time darling of the fickle literati
clapping her hands at the salt and oil,
the blackened seeds of our party.

The Click of the Door

Another creature haunts the condo
like a quiet hangover,
a new lover, a sine qua non.

An ivory Jesus hangs from an invisible cross,
His head to one side,
sad but with a waiting look.
The washer-dryer
rocks in the pantry.
St. Thomas sits at his writing table.

The street sweepers are gone already
and the computer's already on.
My scalp hurts like the morning after.

But it's not the morning after.
It's the morning before.

Missing

The caregivers come and go
but you remain,
appearing at my study door
again and again
with your child's pink smile
as you forget why you're here.
"Just to while away the time," I venture,
patting the couch beside me.
You sit as I work until
the TV draws you back out.
You watch standing up now.
Sometimes I come into a
room and see you standing
for minutes at a time.

All This Time

All this time I've watched your wits leap away
like flying fish ascending. Then today I see that
I'm caught in your dazey wake. You're taking me
along for the ride. I mean a *lot* of me.

All the things about me that you loved or liked
or noticed. All the things that we did together
that you remember but I don't. All the things
I did wrong and all the wonderful, thoughtful,
darling things I did right and how much
you love love love me and how not too long
from now you won't remember me, and I won't
remember the things about us you hold in escrow.
Things about me I can only guess at that you adore:
How my lovemaking invariably brings on *la petite mort*,

how I glance out of the corner of my eye when I joke,
the dear serious expression that fills my face when writing,
the flash of righteous anger in the face of injustice,
my kindness toward those less fortunate than I,
when I saved those children from the tenement fire,
when the Beatles asked me to sit in for Ringo because
he had plantar fasciitis and couldn't pedal the bass,
when I got hit by lightning and lost my hair but acquired
the ability to fly! Without your memories, where will I be?
Coming your way, paddling toward that bright light, or nullity.

Raptor

I woke at three feeling heartless,
not in the sense of cruel, but in a more literal sense—
I felt my heart was missing. Not in a literal sense, really,
more in a metaphorical sense—as if my chest were raked
clean. In the kitchen, I got a glass of water and raised
the blinds and you'll never guess what I saw.
I saw you. You were a crow. It looked like a crow,
it might've been some kind of raptor. It was
a variously blue night, lots of blues, more like
dusk than three in the morning.
You were flying through the gradations
of blue. Even though it was a crow
or possibly some kind of raptor, I could tell it was you.
In its claws was a heart.
I watched it fly—watched you fly—swoop, really,
off with a single cry.

The Evening Wolves

The Eskimos (they say) ship the old lady off on an ice floe.
They don't say if any of these old ladies are named Flo,
but frankly I wouldn't be surprised.
I'm trying to express my anger in healthy ways.

I wonder if they really do that, it seems cruel if convenient.
Hunger is a frightful way to die, poor Florence!
The thought of Flo starving on that chunk of ice as she rocks
across a frigid sea …
Oh … maybe they freeze to death, an easier release.

I'm trying to express my anger in healthy ways.
My fantasies about my 'care-receiver,' whose name—
well, let's call her Flo—
my fantasies run toward the bizarre. I think of a giant slingshot
shooting her into the sky 'til she's dancing with the stars,
happy on her celestial ice floe.

Or she wanders off and a wolf family
takes her in—Flo Mowgli—
and cares for her like their own granny,
singing her to sleep with a wolfish ditty,
soothing her nerves with their rough tongues.

You'll be livin' the life, old sweetheart, and me freed
from the role of burning out caregiver.
The only drawback is how much I'll miss you
up there in the spheres of heaven or down in your
warm furry den with the evening wolves.

Bertha You Are Not

Remember, dear, when you feared
you'd be the woman in the attic?
You turned to me a year ago
when you were scarce half gone,

"I'm afraid I'll be Bertha soon, my God."
But Bertha you are not. You are
a new child drawn to all that glitters,
handing me your rhinestone barrettes

so I can pin them in your burred hair.
You are more afraid and smaller than
you once were. You dance and dance
when the music plays and there is
no way to tell one from the other.

Walking Home

I'm walking home from the convenience store
thinking about an old girlfriend who shape-
shifted into *nü gui* one summer evening
when a stone garden cat gives me the eye
and the creeps. I've got three almond
Hershey bars in my pocket for the mad wife,
and a package of peanut M&M's for me.
The street's dark and cold and when the
wind picks up, I roll myself into a ball
and turn around to avoid the sting, facing
where I've been, the wind at my back
and remember how I dreamt about women again
the night before. I dream about women almost
every night next to her coarse quiet breathing.
And then I remember the scene in *Fargo* where Mike
Yanagita at the Radisson restaurant tries to put up
a good front for Marge Gunderson then falls to pieces,
and Marge delicately lowers her head to her diet Coke.

Your Hair's Sour Scent

Your hair's sour scent
is all that seems the same.
Your gait's gone slow and wary.
Your words scatter like cinders.
Your sadness makes it hard for
me to lift my arms.
On the odd day your eyes know
something I don't know, and don't want to know.
You know where you're going and might just want to go.
It's as if the tide was always low
and the waves receding show the jewels
the sea hides beneath its slick black reeds—
polished stones, scalloped shells, and pearls.

Agador

Bent over your hard feet,
pulling up your starry blue socks
then easing down to my knees
to wrestle you into shoes
with a plastic horn, I hear a
new word from above, "Agador."

"What did you say?" And by then
you don't remember. "Agador?"
I muse aloud and your grateful,
loopy smile cues a voice,
loopy and grateful, in my inner ear.
 "Agador." Silly, devoted Agador.

Rattus Rattus

My heart is in my nose.
My head is full of stones.
Something between a bat and a moth
is adrift in my chest
fluttering up my throat.
Not long ago a rat was scrabbling inside our
bedroom wall. You didn't care. Even your
phobias had fled the marvel that was
once your mind. I slapped the wall
and froze the rat in its tracks.
I sensed his trembling whiskers,
felt his tripping heart. I slapped
the wall again. You mumbled and
turned over. Soon, I slept too
and dreamt of the Pied Piper
and his pitiless song.

Your Words

Your words are clouds, smoke, dry ice.
Your words are slit-eyed frogs. I nod
and whisper in your ear,
"Do you know how much I love you?"

Dancer

You shone white hot
and humans lay like cats 'round
your brazen belly.

You tore through badlands and big-shouldered cities,
through wild women who never got the blues
and all those always-blue men, humming
Hank Snow, drinking bourbon, clutching onto
you like the last reed.

You belly-danced on tables,
waltzed with drunken husbands,
boogie-woogied with their wives.

Now at almost four-score
your face is still pink with embers.
Now you sit mute,
trembling with indecipherable anxieties,
and when asked to dance, you demur.

'Sunshine'

People smile when the sun comes out,
especially in Lake Forest where we met,
you standing in a dappled spot where
maple leaves stirred above, turning
your flushed face dark then light then dark.
"Sunshine" was your mother's name for you.

The whole world smiled as you
strolled with me out of the shade.
You were dazzling. Sometimes
I had to cover my eyes.

The dark grew in you like evening,
the dark grew in you like night. Now,
you stutter out dark bullets instead of words.
But you still love to sit in the afternoon light
while I watch you fold into your own shadow.

It's a Strange Thing

It's a strange thing to enter a strange room
In a home you've lived in for years.
There are times now I don't know where I am.

My pockets have holes, their holes have holes.
They leak thoughts like dimes. It's odd;
Such a strange thing to enter a strange room.

Sew the holes in my pockets with black thread
So I can remember even the dark dreams, for
I'm afraid right now I don't know how I can.

Tell me again about the mourning doves,
How they whir when they fly away.
What an odd thing (in your own home!) to enter a strange room.

Tell me about the doves one more time.
I'll hold them near in my mind and heart;
Forgive me, dear, I don't know who you are.

Tell me about how we met and where,
And I'll fill my pockets with souvenirs.
It's a strange thing to enter a strange room.
I'm afraid right now I don't know where I am.

Do Not Forsake Me

I know that I'll forsake you, oh,
my darling, but I'm not sure when
I'll drive you through the riven
world to suites in fluorescent rows,

medicine air, mortal stench and
good green nurses. Not sure how
I'll wave goodbye to you, silent
in bleached light on a long bench

and leave us both alone,
me to remember, you to
continue to forget. And you
might just wave back, old crone,

old pal, girl of all my dreams
(mostly nightmares, this last year,
when the sweet ones spurred tears and
bad dreams, you might say, reigned supreme).

And back home, what then? Will I, wild
in the weird quiet, tear from the walls
the paintings of woods and waterfalls
that reminded you of country calm

and remind me only of your
long descent into less and less
'til you saw neither forest
nor trees; and the flora you

once distinguished like a botanist
became just other bits of chaos
to thwart your lost, courageous
war on terror and lawlessness?

Or will I, more likely I'm afraid,
swoon onto our bed and stay there
'til the seasons change, 'til I hear
birds sing again, then birdsong fade?

Blight

You see me, the quick tears come,
and I resist the urge to flee.
Decades of dry-eyed practicality
accustomed me to the sweet serene:
the hatted gardener turning over loam,
the eternal jeans—one tear in a knee,
the second I'd spy out the window to see
as you bent to dislodge some stubborn stone.
Until one day (one night?) synapses start
to misfire, growing webcaps of plaque
instead of parsley, lady slippers, soapwort.
Your agile mind gets stranded in the muck
and soon you're all need, and for my part,
I learn to serve, getting nothing back.

In the Penal Colony

They use a two-pronged apparatus
to lift her in a sort of hammock
from bed to wheeled chair
where she sleeps sitting
until they bring the device back
two hours later to raise and rest her
on the bed to sleep lying.

Several sailorless parrots perch
in a cage, beaks buried in their feathers
until they wake fouling and squawking.
Yesterday a woman howled the whole
long day, drowning out the birds
and frightening the horses, although
the lifers and nurses seemed unfazed.

The man with the clean athletic sock
on the stump of his absent forearm
rolls chuckling down the linoleum halls.

Parting

Every time we say goodbye,
she traces my face with spastic fingers,
tentatively touches my forehead,
the tip of my nose, and the lines
running down to my mouth.

Pollyanna

"Death comes unexpectedly!" roared the pastor
before the young girl softened his heart. And so do tears,
as his did after the young girl softened his heart.
As mine do when, at the front of a grocery line,
I think of you in that strange place, in a strange
mind, enduring an end nobody deserves.
Especially you, who once helped me believe,
but now, how, I think, could Anyone do this to you?
Or anyone? "Are you OK?" asks the frightened clerk.

Friends like You
    After George Herbert's 'Confession'

Sorrow, you savvy son of a bitch!
No matter how high the wall,
how strait the gate
how devious the diversions,
you're in like Flynn.

No Olympic diver, no hot
knife through butter,
no tent-slipping Judith
equals grief's cunning silence,
the thief who stays the night

and wakes you in the morning
saying "What's for breakfast?"
then sits on your stomach like
a bad meal before the long day
brings back the dark.

Some say—social workers,
therapists, poets and priests of all faiths—
that if sorrow isn't shunned but
embraced as a friend,
with time its power will fade.

But you're too smart for that.

Barbecue

In the patio garden,
there's phlox, daylilies, larkspur,
walkers, wheelchairs,
and a billowing grill.

I hold your hand
as you lift into the sky like smoke.

Alec Solomita has worked as an illustrator, editor, critic, fiction writer, and poet. He graduated *summa cum laude* from Amherst College in 1989 and went on to pursue a Ph.D. at Princeton (he didn't catch it).

For several years, Solomita worked as a freelance critic, his reviews and essays appearing in *The New Republic, The Boston Globe, The New Criterion, The Wall Street Journal*, and elsewhere. His fiction has appeared in, among other publications, *The Adirondack Review, The Mississippi Review, Southwest Review* and Ireland's *Southword Journal*. He's published poetry in *3Elements Literary Review, Literary Orphans, Turk's Head Review, MadHatLit*, and many other venues. He's been shortlisted by the *Bridport Prize* and *Southword Journal* and named a finalist by the *Noctua Review*. He studied poetry under the acute eyes of Katia Kapovich, John Canaday, and Frannie Lindsay.

He worked as editor and illustrator at the *Harvard Gazette* for over a decade until he left the job to care for his ailing wife, Joan Chase, author of the recently re-released, much-celebrated novel *During The Reign of the Queen of Persia* (NYRB Classics).

Do Not Forsake Me—a gentle, fierce, lyrical telling of his wife's, courageous struggle with dementia and Parkinson's disease—is Solomita's first chapbook.

www.ingramcontent.com/pod-product-compliance
Lightning Source LLC
LaVergne TN
LVHW041515070426
835507LV00012B/1595